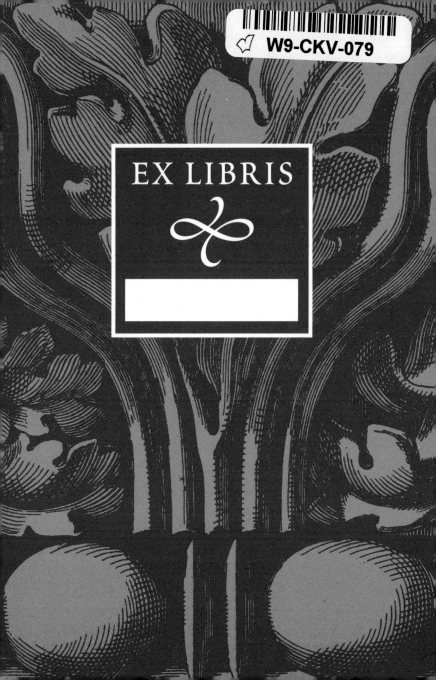

EX LIBRIS

NOTA BENE

NOTA BENE

A Guide to Familiar Latin Quotes and Phrases

EDITED BY

ROBIN LANGLEY SOMMER

PAST TIMES®

IN MEMORIAM
MARYELLEN ABLEY

Copyright © 1995, DoveTail Books

Special Edition for
PAST TIMES®
Oxford, England

First published in this edition in Great Britain in 1996.

Design copyright © Ziga Design

Produced in association with Saraband Inc.

ISBN 0-9636673-7-8

Printed in China

9 8 7 6 5 4 3

Contents

Foreword

*N*ow that the study of classical languages has become less common than it was a hundred years ago, many educated English-speaking people welcome a succinct guide to the Latin roots of their language. Perhaps half of all English words in current use are of Latin origin, and it is inseparable from the study of the Romance languages: French, Italian, Spanish, Portuguese, and Romanian. In addition, the great writers of Roman civilisation have left their imprint on these living languages in the form of quotations, maxims, anecdotes, figures of speech, and ideas that are still germane and powerful almost 2,000 years later. Through all its phases of development, from the pre-literary Latin of ancient Italy through the Medieval Latin of European schools and monasteries that preserved the classical heritage, Latin has endured as a language of rare beauty and precision, colouring our lives in ways we may not even be aware of. In the realm of language, all roads do, indeed, lead to Rome.

∴ I ∴

Familiar
Quotations &
Inscriptions

Idioms: Latin Everyone Knows

Ad hoc
For this particular purpose
(common usage: improvise)

Ad captandum vulgus
To appeal to the crowd

Ad hominem
To the person (to appeal to feelings
rather than reason)

Ad libitum (ad lib)
Freely; at pleasure

Alea iacta est
The die is cast

Alter ego
Another self

Amicus curiae
Friend of the court (objective adviser)

Ars gratia artis
Art for art's sake

Ars longa, vita brevis
Art is long, life is short

Bona fide
In good faith

Carpe diem
Sieze the day
(make the most of the opportunity)

Cave canem
Beware of the dog!

Caveat emptor
Let the buyer beware

Ceteris paribus
Other things being equal

Circa
About, approximately

Cogito ergo sum
I think, therefore I am
(Descartes, *seventeenth century*)

Cui bono
Whom does it benefit?

Cum grano salis
With a grain of salt

De novo
Anew

Deus ex machina
An improbable solution, artificially introduced
to resolve a difficulty or untangle a dramatic plot

Divide et impera
Divide and rule

E pluribus unum
From many, one

Ecce homo
Behold the man!

Emeritus
Honorary; by reason of merit

Errare humanum est
To err is human

Ex animo
From the heart; sincerely

Ex libris
From the books of
(from the library of)

Ex post facto
After the fact

Fortes fortuna juvat
Fortune favours the brave

Hic jacet _____
Here lies _____

Habeas corpus
A legal writ to end unlawful restraint
by bringing a prisoner into court

In memoriam
In memory of

In toto
Altogether

In vino veritas
In wine is truth

Lapsus linguae
A slip of the tongue

Lapsus memoriae
A slip of the memory

Magna cum laude
With great honour

Magnum opus
Masterpiece (a great work)

Mea culpa
My fault

Mens sana in corpore sano
Sound of body, sound of mind

Mirabile dictu
Wonderful to tell

Multum in parvo
Much in a little

Naturo abhorret a vacuo
Nature abhors a vacuum

Nolens volens
Whether willing or not (willy-nilly)

Noli me tangere
Let nothing touch me (do not interfere)

Non compos mentis
Of unsound mind

Non sequitur
A statement that does not follow
logically from what preceded it

Omnia vincit amor
Love conquers all

Pax vobiscum
Peace be with you

Per annum
Per year

Per capita
Per head

Pro bono publico
For the public good

Pro tempore
For the time being
(temporarily)

Persona non grata
An unpleasing person

Quid pro quo
A thing for a thing (substitute)

Quieta non movere
Do not move settled things
(let sleeping dogs lie)

Sapere aude
Dare to be wise

Status quo
The existing state of affairs

Summum bonum
The supreme good

Summum ius summa inuria
The more law, the less justice

Tabula rasa
A clean slate

Terra firma
Solid ground

Terra incognita
An unknown land

Usus est magister optimus
Practice makes perfect

Via
By way of

Via media
The middle path

Vice versa
With the order or
meaning reversed

Vox populi, vox dei
The voice of the people is
the voice of God

Familiar Mottoes

Ave Atque Vale
Hail and Farewell!

De Mortuis Nil Nisi Bonum
Let Nothing But Good Be Said of the Dead

Dominus Illuminatio Mea
May the Lord Guide Me

Dum Spiro, Spero
While I Breathe, I Hope

Esto Perpetua
It Is Everlasting

Excelsior
Ever Upward!

Labor Omnia Vincit
Labour Conquers All Things

Justitia Omnibus
Justice to All

Nil Sine Numini
Nothing Without Providence

Per Ardua Ad Astra
Through Hardship to the Stars

Regnat Populus
The People Rule

Semper Fidelis
Always Faithful

Semper Paratus
Always Prepared

Sic Semper Tyrannis
Thus Always to Tyrants

Expressions from Roman Drama

Plautus (ca. 251–184 BC)

A WORD TO THE WISE

SATURIO Here I am! Hope I didn't keep you waiting.

TOXILUS Go on, get over there far off and out of sight,
   and be silent;

When you see me talking to the pimp—

A word to the wise is enough.

  —*THE PERSIAN*, ACT 4, SC. 7, li. 726–27

WHOM THE GODS LOVE DIES YOUNG

CHRYSALUS Whom the gods love

Dies young; yet he lives—breathes—is conscious.

If any god loved this man, he should have died

More than ten, no, more than twenty years ago.

He burdens the ground as he walks, already senseless

And witless, worth about as much as a stinking mush-
   room.

  —*THE TWO BACCHISES*, ACT 4, SC. 7, li. 816–821

Terence (ca. 195–159 BC)

FORTUNE FAVOURS THE BRAVE

ANTIPHO Wretched me! How can I find a remedy for this
sudden ruin?
For if it is my fortune, Phanium, to be divided from
you,
Life is no longer desirable to me.

GETA Now that it is so, Antipho,
So much the more ought you be watchful: fortune
favours the brave.

—*PHORMIO*, ACT I, SC. 3, li. 201–203

NOTHING IS SAID THAT HAS NOT BEEN SAID BEFORE

He doesn't deny that in his *Eunuch* he has transported
characters out of the Greek; but…if the same characters
will not be permitted, how is it more permissible to depict
a servant on the run, or to make use of good old women,
evil courtesans, a gluttonous parasite, a braggart soldier,
a changeling, an old man duped by a servant, or even
love, hate, and suspicion? In short, nothing is said that
has not been said before.

—*THE EUNUCH*, PROL., li. 31–41

Expressions from Roman Poetry

Horace (65–8 BC)

THE GOLDEN MEAN
aurea mediocritas

Whoever is content with the golden mean
Is safe from the squalor
Of a ruined home, and temperately avoids
A house that provokes envy.

—ODES, Bk 2, Ode 10, li. 5–8

SEIZE THE DAY
carpe diem

Be wise, strain your wine, and in this brief space
Cut back long hopes. Even as we speak, envious time
Flees: seize the day, trust little in tomorrow.

—ODES, Bk I, Ode 11, li. 6–8

Expressions from Roman History

BREAD AND CIRCUSES

Long since, because we can sell our votes to no one,
We have thrown off our cares; those who once bestowed
Rule, the *fasces*, legions, everything, now refrain,
And hunger for only two things:
Bread and circuses.

—Juvenal, "Tenth Satire," li. 78–82

*This phrase is used in a political context to refer to the basic
necessities to keep the people content, to win votes.*

A PYRRHIC VICTORY

According to some accounts, when one of his men rejoiced
at the victory they had won, Pyrrhus gave this answer:
"If we win another of the price, we are utterly undone."

—Plutarch, *Life of Pyrrhus*, ch. 21

*A victory whose cost is so great as to negate its value is
referred to as Pyrrhic.*

THE SABINE WOMEN

Many people gathered at Rome, for they were eager to see the new city…Even the Sabines came, and brought their wives and children with them….

When the time had come for the spectacles, and the visitors' eyes and minds were all fixed upon them, then the Romans sprang their plot; upon a given signal, the Roman youths broke out to seize the virgins.

—LIVY, *THE HISTORY OF ROME*, BK I, CH 9

The Sabines, from the Umbrian region of Italy, were ancestors of the ancient Romans. This scene was said to have occurred during the founding of Rome by Romulus.

TO CROSS THE RUBICON

Now when Caesar had overtaken his cohorts at the river Rubicon, which was the utmost boundary of his province, he rested for a while; then, considering how great an enterprise he was undertaking, turned to those who stood next to him and said, "As yet, friends, we are able to turn back; but once we pass over this little bridge, there will be no business but by force of arms and dint of sword."

—SUETONIUS, *THE DEIFIED JULIUS*, PARA. 31

In modern usage, this phrase refers to an irrevocable decision or an action with far-reaching consequences.

I CAME, I SAW, I CONQUERED

Having finished all his wars, Caesar rode in five triumphs: four times in the same month, with a few days between each triumph, after vanquishing Scipio; and once again after he had overcome the children of Pompey…In his Pontic triumph, amidst the pageants and pomp, he caused to be carried before him an inscription of these three words: *Veni, vidi, vici*; and this signified, not the outcome of the war, which other conquerors would have celebrated, but rather his speed in dispatching the war.

—Suetonius, *The Deified Julius*, para. 37

Caesar's most famous motto.

TO TAKE WITH A GRAIN OF SALT

In the chambers of the great king Mithridaes, Cneius Pompeius discovered in a private notebook, in the king's own hand, the formula for an antidote: two dry nuts, the same number of figs, and twenty leaves of rue ground together, with a grain of salt added; whoever took this on an empty stomach would be harmed by no poison that day.

—Pliny the Elder, *Natural History*, Bk 23, ch 77

A cautionary note to take something as doubtful, the phrase is a comment on the effectiveness of Pliny's recipe as an antidote to poison.

Gods of Roman Mythology

Jupiter

The sky god, associated with the Greek god Zeus. Jupiter was seen as the source of Roman civic greatness and military might, and made his opinions known by the use of weather signs, especially thunder and lightning.

Juno

Jupiter's consort, she was considered responsible for all aspects of women's lives and affairs.

Janus

The first and oldest of the Roman gods; he guarded entrances and exits, bridges and boundaries. On Roman coins he is portrayed symbolically with two faces.

Mars

The god of war. Sacrifices were offered to him before and after battles. He was originally an agricultural god and is associated with both the wolf and the woodpecker.

Minerva

Goddess of the intellect and the arts, associated with the Greek goddess Athena. She was patroness of craftsmen, authors, educators, painters, and schoolchildren.

~ II ~

For Bookworms & Scholars

Great Latin Authors

C. Julius Caesar
C. 100–44 BC

Charismatic statesman, strategist, and general, as well as historian.

C. Valerius Catullus
1ST CENTURY BC

Lyric poet and member of Rome's literary and political élites. His poems primarily describe his unhappy love affair with Clodia (whom he referred to as Lesbia).

M. Porcius Cato
234–149 BC

Orator, politician, and historian whose manual on farming is the earliest known surviving work in Latin prose.

M. Tullius Cicero
106–43 BC

Orator, writer, and philosopher. His detailed letters are a crucial source of our knowledge of contemporary Roman life; his rhetorical and philosophical works were highly influential in his time.

Q. Ennius
239–169 BC
Early Roman poet best known for his epic historical poem the *Annales* and for his tragedies based on Greek drama.

Horace
65–8 BC
Satirist, critic, and lyric poet.

D. Junius Juvenalis (Juvenal)
1ST-2ND CENTURY AD
Satirical poet who exposed the decadence of Roman society under Emperor Domitian.

T. Livius (Livy)
59 BC–AD 17
The Roman Empire's greatest historian, author of the 142-volume *History of Rome*.

T. Lucretius Carus
1ST CENTURY BC
Poet and Epicurean philosopher whose works include *De Rerum Natura*—literally translated as *On Natural Things,* but concerning legend and mythology.

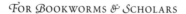

P. Ovidius Naso (Ovid)

43 BC–C. AD 17

One of ancient Rome's most prolific poets, whose risqué
Ars amatoria caused Augustus to send him into exile. In
addition to love poetry, he wrote on the theme of mythology in *Metamorphoses.*

Phaedrus

C. 15 BC–C. AD 50

Author of fables written in verse, which were modelled
on Aesop's fables.

T. Maccius Plautus

C. 254–184 BC

Dramatist who was the author of more than fifty come-
dies. Shakespeare's *Comedy of Errors* was based on Plautus's
Menaechmi.

C. Plinius Secundus maior (Pliny the Elder)

C. AD 23–79

Scientist and historian whose surviving works cover natural history, astronomy, and geography. Pliny's curiosity
led him to die of asphyxiation watching the eruption of
Mount Vesuvius at close range.

C. Plinius Caecilius Secundus minor (Pliny the Younger)

C. AD 61–110

Prolific letter-writer whose vivid description provides the best surviving account of the eruption of Vesuvius.

C. Sallustius Crispus (Sallust)

86–C. 34 BC

Historian who wrote in epigrammatic form.

L. Annaeus Seneca

C. 4 BC–AD 65

Philosopher, playwright (chiefly of tragedies) and essayist.

Cornelius Tacitus

C. AD 55–120

Orator, statesman, and historian whose works include *Annales, Historiae* and *Life of Agricola.*

P. Vergilius Maro (Virgil)

70–19 BC

Pastoral poet, author of the *Aeneid,* considered the greatest Latin poem.

Standard Latin Abbreviations

A.U.C.
Anno urbis conditae (reckoned from 753 BC)
from the founding of the city [of Rome]

A.D.
Ante diem (in dates)
Before the day

COS.
Consul
One of the two chief magistrates of the
Roman state under the republic

E.Q.R.
Eques Romanus
the Roman cavalry

F.
Filius; fecit
Son; made by

G.
Gallica; Germania
Pertaining to Gaul; Germany

H.S.E.
Hic situs est
This is the place

ID.
Idus
the Ides—In the Roman calendar,
the 15th day of March, May, July, and October;
the 13th day of the other months

IMP.
Imperium, imperator
Imperial; emperor

L.
Locus; libra
Place; book (as numeral, 50)

M.
Mille
1,000

P.C.
Patres conscripti
The senators enrolled
(title of the assembled Senate)

P.M.
Pontifex Maximus
High Priest

P.P.
Pater patriae
The father of the nation

Q.E.D.
Quod erat demonstrandum
That which is demonstrated or proved

R.P.
Res publica
Public affairs

S.P.Q.R.
Senatus populusque Romanus
The Senate and the people of Rome

Unusual Word Derivations

ANTLER
from *antocularis*: before the eye

BUGLE
from *buculus*: a young bull

CHAPEL
from *capella*: cloak

PAY
from *pacare*: to make peace

SOLDIER
from *solidus*: a gold coin

SULLEN
from *solus*: alone

VILLAIN
from *villanus*: farm hand

Scholarly Usage

AD LIB.
ad libitum, at will

AD LOC.
ad locum, at the place

BIBL.
bibliotheca, library

C./CA.
circa, about; approximately

CF.
confer, compare

CON.
contra, against

E.G.
exempli gratia, for example

ETC.
et cetera, and so forth

FL.
floruit, flourished

IBID.
ibidem, in the same place

I.E.
id est, that is

M.M.
mutatis mutandis, necessary changes being made

MS/MSS
manuscriptum, -a, manuscript(s)

N.B.
nota bene, take careful note

OP. CIT.
opere citato, in the work cited

PASS.
passim, throughout

Q.V.
quod vide, which see

Latin Words Adopted Directly into English

ADMINISTRATOR	LEGION
APPENDIX	LYNX
AQUEDUCT	MAJOR
ATRIUM	ORATOR
AUXILIARY	ORCHESTRA
CENSOR	SECTOR
COHORT	SEPIA
CONSENSUS	SIMULACRUM
CREATOR	TORPOR
CURRICULUM	TRIUMVIRATE
DICTATOR	TUBA
EDUCATOR	ULTRA
FORUM	UXORIOUS
GLADIATOR	VERNACULAR
IBIS	VIADUCT

~ III ~

Time in
its Flight

The Julian Calendar: 46 BC

January
For Janus, the two-faced god and doorkeeper, who knew the past and foresaw the future. In his shrine, the doors were closed in times of peace and open in times of war.

February
From *februare*, to expiate or purify, for the mid-month feast of Lupercus, god of fertility. With January, it was added to Rome's original ten-month Alban calendar after 738 BC.

March
For Mars, the god of war. The wolf, a raiding animal, was sacred to him and closely connected to Rome's legendary founders, Romulus and Remus. During March, the priests of Mars paraded the city with the god's sacred shield.

April
From *Aperio*, I open, for the springtime burgeoning of nature, regarded as the true beginning of the year in agricultural societies.

May
Linked both to Maia, the goddess of growth and increase, and *Maiores*, the senate in Rome's original constitution.

June
For Juno, queen of the gods and guardian of women, which gave rise to the belief that June was the most auspicious month for marriages.

July
For Julius Caesar (Gaius Julius), who reformed the Roman calendar with advice from the astrologer Sosigenes (by their era, it was about three months ahead of the schedule fixed by the seasons).

August
For Augustus (Octavian), Julius Caesar's adopted son and the first Roman emperor (27 BC). His reign marked the beginning of the *Pax Romana*, or Roman Peace, which lasted for 200 years.

September, October, November, & December
Named for their numerical order in the original ten-month calendar as the year's seventh, eighth, ninth, and tenth months.

The Seasons

The Romans adopted their explanation for the change from winter to summer from the Greeks, changing the names of the principal characters according to their own mythology:

Ceres

The goddess of agriculture had a home on Mount Olympus but preferred her cottage on Earth, from which she sowed the seeds in springtime, oversaw the growth of grain and fruit all summer, and blessed the harvests in the autumn.

Proserpina

Ceres' beautiful daughter had charge of all the flowers, which sprang up in her footsteps wherever she walked. She tended them with her companions and gathered them for wreaths.

Pluto

The dour god of the underworld kidnapped Proserpina from her fields and took her to his dark subterranean world to be his wife. She pined there while Ceres searched the Earth for her and appealed for help to the other gods.

Mercury

The gods' wing-footed messenger traveled to Pluto's realm to announce that the Fates had decreed that Proserpina could return to the light of day only if she had eaten nothing underground. He was grieved to hear that Proserpina had eaten a few of the seeds of a pomegranate.

The Fates

The arbiters of destiny relented and decreed that Proserpina could return to her mother on Earth for two-thirds of the year but must spend the rest of her time in the underworld. Thus no flowers bloomed and no seeds sprouted during the winter months of her exile.

Timely Words and Phrases

Ab ovo usque ad mala
From the beginning to the end (of the feast):
From the egg to the apples

Ad infinitum
Endlessly: **infinity**

Ad tempus
For the time being: **temporary**

Aeternus
Everlasting: **eternal**

Annus
A year (a circuit of the sun): **annual**

Centesimus
The hundredth: **centennial**

Dictum factum
No sooner said than done

Dies
Day: **daily**

Diu
By day: **diurnal**

Exigua pars est vitae quam nos vivimus
The part of life we really live is short (Seneca)

Ex post facto
After the fact

Festina lente
Make haste slowly (Augustus)

Interim
Meanwhile: **interval**

Luna
The moon: **lunar**

Meminerunt omnia amantes
Lovers remember everything (Ovid)

Nox
Night: **nocturnal**

Nunc aut nunquam
Now or never

Post mortem
After death

Praemonitus praemunitus
Forewarned, forearmed

Prima lux
Dawn: **first light**

Sol
The sun: **solar**

Tempus fugit
Time flies

Timekeeping

The ancients first told time by the marked-off shadows of trees, which led to the creation of the sundial. To measure time at night or on overcast days, the Romans used the water clock, or *clepsydra*, which was also known to the Egyptians, Greeks, and Chinese. The volume of water flowing from one vessel to another was measured to mark the passage of time, similar to the movement of sand in an hourglass. Roman numerals are still used for the faces of clocks and to record dates on monuments and public buildings.

Timeline of the Roman Republic and Empire

753 BC The founding of Rome; the joining of the Seven Hills of Rome.

509 BC Roman Republic era begins.

60 BC Julius Caesar, Marcus Crassus and Pompey form the First Triumvirate.

46 BC Caesar becomes dictator of Rome.

27 BC Augustus Caesar becomes emperor, ending the Republican era.

AD 79 Pompeii destroyed by eruption of Vesuvius.

AD 98–117 The Roman Empire reaches its greatest extent during the reign of Trajan.

AD 284–305 The Roman Empire is divided into Eastern and Western sections during the reign of Diocletian; considered the beginning of the end of the Empire.

AD 476 Romulus Augustus, last Western emperor, is defeated. The Eastern Empire continues as the Byzantine Empire.

∻ IV ∻

The Romance of Language

Expressions and Idioms from Nature

DOG DAYS

"Who does not know that the solar fires are excited at the rising of the dog-star [Sirius, in August], whose effect is great and is felt on Earth?…Undoubtedly, dogs are most likely to be rabid during the whole of this time."

—Pliny the Elder, *Natural History*

Pliny's vast encyclopedia in thirty-seven volumes was studded with popular stories—(and errors)—collected on his extensive travels through the Roman Empire, of which the following is an example:

IN A NUTSHELL

"There are examples of sharpness of vision that are quite incredible. Cicero reports that there was a copy of Homer's *Iliad* [24 books] inscribed on a piece of parchment enclosed in a nutshell."

A RARE BIRD

Is there no one among these crowds who
    seems deserving to you?
Let her be beautiful, becoming, rich, and
    fertile; let her place
Ancient ancestors in her galleries;
    let her be more chaste
Than all the Sabine women, with dishevelled hair,
    who broke off the war:
A rare bird, as rare on Earth as a black swan;
Who could bear a wife so possessed of
    all things?

—Juvenal, *Sixth Satire*

*Black swans were unknown to the Romans, so when Juvenal
wrote "rare," he meant nonexistent.*

ANOTHER RARE BIRD

A Happy Man Is Rarer Than a White Crow.

This popular saying was rendered: Felix ille tamen corvo
quoque rarior albo.

TO LEAD BY THE NOSE

"The only certain ground for discovering truth is the faculty of discriminating false from true, distinguishing the sound and genuine from the base and counterfeit, as the silver assayers do with coins. When you have at last managed to acquire such a faculty, then you may investigate the [Stoic] doctrines. Otherwise, I can assure you, you will be led by the nose by anyone who chooses to do it, and you will run after anything they hold out to you, as cattle do after a green bough."

—LUCIAN, *HERMOTIMUS*

A SNAKE IN THE GRASS

A dialogue between two rustic poets, which Virgil used to attack his critics, Bavius and Maevius, and to flatter his patron, Pollio:

DAMOETAS May he who loves you, Pollio, come to share in our fame; Let honey flow, and the harsh bramble-bush yield balsam.

MENALCAS Let him, Maevius, that does not hate Bavius, love your songs, And let him also yoke foxes and milk the he-goats.

DAMOETAS May you who gather flowers and strawberries from the ground, Flee, you children, from the cold snake hiding in the grass.

—"THIRD ECLOGUE," LINES 88–93

WATER FROM A STONE

A dialogue between two slaves, one of whom is in love and needs money:

TOXILUS You can make me your everlasting friend.

SAGARISO How?

TOXILUS By giving me sixty silver coins so that I may buy her freedom, which I will pay back immediately, in three days' time, or four. Be a true friend and help me out.

SAGARISO What arrogance, to dare asking me for so much money! Even if I sold my whole self, I would scarcely get enough to cover it. You're asking for water from a pumice stone that's thirsty itself.

—PLAUTUS, *THE PERSIAN*, ACT 1, SCENE 1

TO ADD INSULT TO INJURY

A fly bit the bare head of a bald man, who, trying to swat it, gave himself a slap. Then the fly said, laughing, "You would avenge the bite of so small a creature by killing him; and so you would add insult to injury by striking yourself?"…

—PHAEDRUS, "THE BALD MAN AND THE FLY"

A COUNTRY MOUSE (HORACE) TAUNTS A CITY MOUSE

If it behooves us to live according to nature,
And seeking a site to build a house is our first task,
Then what place could be more splendid than the
    country?…
Even you, amid your varied columns, nurse a forest
And praise a house with a prospect on distant fields.
You may cast out nature with a pitchfork, yet it will
    always return,
And stealthily break through your stupid disdain,
    victorious."

—*EPISTLES*, BOOK 1, EPISTLE 10

A Rolling Stone Gathers No Moss
Attributed to the Roman actor Pubilius Syrus,
first century BC

A Blackbird Always Sits Close to a Blackbird
The antecedent of our "Birds of a Feather
Flock Together"

Beware of the Silent Dog And Still Water
Both were dangerous

An Ass at the Lyre Like Bees at Geometry
Two Roman insults

To Hold the Wolf by the Ears
As in "the bull by the horns"

With Claws and Beak
"Tooth and nail"

YOU CAN LEAD A HORSE TO WATER, BUT YOU CANNOT MAKE HIM DRINK

From *stultitia est venatum ducere invitas canes* (Plautus)

NO SMOKE WITHOUT FIRE

semper flamma fumo proxima (Plautus)

TO SWIM AGAINST THE TIDE

From *contra terrentem bracchia dirigere* (Juvenal)

ALL THAT LIVES COMES FROM THE EGG

omne vivum ex ovo

EVERY CLOUD HAS A SILVER LINING

From *inter vepres rosae nascuntur*

TO ERR IS HUMAN

Errare humanum est (Cicero)

Figures of Speech from Virgil

A sad thing is a wolf in the fold, rain on ripe corn, wind in the trees, the anger of Amaryllis.

As long as rivers shall run down to the sea, or shadows touch the mountain slopes, or stars graze in the vault of heaven, so long shall your honour, your name, your praises endure.

But meanwhile Neptune saw the ocean's waving commotion…and he summoned the winds, by name. "What arrogance is this, what pride of birth, you winds, to meddle here without my sanction, raising all this trouble? I'll—No the waves come first! but listen to me. You are going to pay for this!"

Arms and the man I sing.

Let us die, and rush into the heart of the fight.

The grove of Angita lamented you,
The glassy watered Fuccinus lamented you,
All limpid lakes lamented you.

Roman Humour

WHEN THE CATS FALL ASLEEP,
THE MOUSE REJOICES
AND LEAPS FROM HIS HOLE
Dum felis dormit, mus gaudet et exsilit antro
(The amusing French variation tells us that "When the
cat's away, the mice will dance on the table")

WHAT A WOMAN SAYS TO
HER FOND LOVER SHOULD
BE WRITTEN ON AIR
OR THE SWIFT WATER
Mulier cupido quod dicit amanti,
In vento et rapida scribere oportet aqua
CATULLUS

THERE'S NOTHING MORE
CONTEMPTIBLE THAN A BALD MAN
WHO PRETENDS TO HAVE HAIR
Calvo turpius est nihil compto
MARTIAL

IF FAME COMES AFTER DEATH, I'M IN NO HURRY FOR IT
Si post fata venit gloria non propero
MARTIAL

THERE IS NOTHING SO ABSURD AS NOT TO HAVE BEEN SAID BY A PHILOSOPHER
Nihil tam absurdum, quod non dictum sit ab aliquo
CICERO

THERE IS NOTHING MORE FRIENDLY THAN A FRIEND IN NEED
Nihil homini amico est opportuno amicius
PLAUTUS

NOTHING IS SILLIER THAN A SILLY LAUGH
Risu inepto res ineptior nulla est
CATULLUS

A BAD VASE DOESN'T BREAK
Malum vas non frangitur

Traits and Qualities

BACCHANALIAN
from Bacchus, god of wine

BELLICOSE
from Bellona, goddess of war

CENSORIOUS
from the Roman office of Censor of Public Morals

HERCULEAN
from Hercules, the hero who won immortality
by strength

INTEGRITY
from *integritas*, soundness

JUNOESQUE
from Juno, queen of the gods

LEGAL
from *legalis*, pertaining to law

LUCULLAN
from Lucullus, wealthy Roman general and gourmet

MERCURIAL
from Mercury, swift messenger of the gods

PATRICIAN
from *patricius*, member of a noble Roman family

PLEBEIAN
from *plebeius*, common people

SATURNINE
from Saturn, the gloomy god of agriculture

SYLVAN
from *sylva*, woods

STELLAR
from *stella*, star

UNDULANT
from *unda*, wave

Latin in the Garden

*T*he Swedish botanist Carolus Linnaeus (18th century) made it possible for gardeners everywhere to do what they like best: talk and write about their favourite plants. His binomial system of classification gave each plant two names: the first, for the genus, is usually Greek; the second, for the species, Latin:

Achillea ageratifolia
YARROW

Baptisia australia
BLUE WILD INDIGO

Campanula carpatica
BELLFLOWER

Delphinium belladonna
LARKSPUR

Filipendula palmata
MEADOWSWEET

Gypsophila paniculata
BABY'S BREATH

Helleborus niger
CHRISTMAS ROSE

Kniphofia
TRITOMA/RED HOT POKER

Lavendula angustifolia
LAVENDER

Nepeta x faassenii
CATMINT

Papaver orientale
ORIENTAL POPPY

Stachys byzantian
LAMB'S EARS

Veronica latifolia
SPEEDWELL

Yucca filamentosa
YUCCA/DESERT CANDLE

Finis

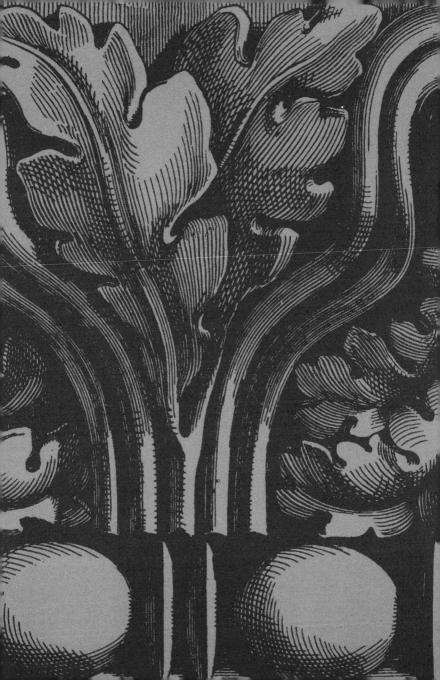